SUZI S

ENCY
FORMULA

THE
CON SIST

Copyright © 2022 by Suzi Sung

All rights reserved. No part of this publication may be reproduced, distributed, or transmitted in any form or by any means, including photocopying, recording, or other electronic or mechanical methods, without the prior written permission of the publisher, except in the case of brief quotations embodied in critical reviews and certain other noncommercial uses permitted by copyright law.

Book Design by HMDpublishing

Contents

Introduction 4

Inconsistency 6

The Comfort Zone 9

The Ego 14
    Ego Excuses 16
    Procrastination 17

The Formula 32
    Goals and Habits 37
    Plan, plan, plan 42
    Proving Yourself Wrong 50
    Learning To Trust 53

One Week Plan 60

Staying Motivated 71

Summary 80

Introduction

Consistency is one of the key components when it comes to reaching your goals because when you are consistent, you will keep doing something regardless of what is going on around you. In other words, you don't just give up whenever things get a little tough in your life or when you just don't feel like doing them.

It's pretty simple when you think about it – keep doing something until you get to where you want to be. However, it's not always easy to execute. If it was, everyone would have reached their goals and be living the life they want to, but they're not.

Most of us have at least one goal we'd like to achieve but haven't yet. It could be that you have started and stopped several times or that you haven't started at all. Whatever the reason, lack of consistency is usually the first explanation for why things haven't worked out. Some people will put this down to the fact that they don't have it in them and that they are not like other people, but anyone can become more consistent with the right tools and methods. In this book, I am going to teach you my tried and true formula for staying on track, doing the work and achieving anything you set your mind to.

This formula will help you to remove self-doubt, build better habits and stop giving up on things so easily. You can finally reach the goals you set!

I'll also share tips on how to stop procrastinating and help you get started in achieving your goals, meaning you won't just finish this book and go back to your life as it was before.

But before we go into the method, I believe it is important to understand what causes inconsistency and what makes you want to give up in the first place. Because when you understand the reasons why you give up, it makes it a lot easier to address them.

Inconsistency

WHAT CAUSES INCONSISTENCY?

The main contributor to your lack of consistency, and the thing that affects pretty much everything you do, comes down to your subconscious beliefs.

These are core beliefs you have about yourself, which are rooted deep within your mind. They create what we call your self-image or your inner story. These beliefs are like an internal affirmation that is always on repeat, and an affirmation in its simplest form is a statement that you declare to be the truth.

Within the subconscious mind, we have lots of these internal affirmations – some good and some not-so-good.

All of our actions are based on these core beliefs and they dictate the choices we make. They are responsible for how we come to decisions, how we react to situations as well as how we feel about ourselves. They are a big factor in how we act and how we choose to live our lives.

Something to understand about these beliefs, and the self-image that is created from them, is that your decisions and actions will always be aligned with them, whether you are aware of it or not. In other words, whatever you try to do in the outside world will always reflect what is going on inside of you. So, even if there is something you really want to have or do, if having or doing it contradicts your self-image, you will unknowingly find a way to stop yourself from having/doing it.

This is when your beliefs become self-limiting beliefs, because they cause you to stop yourself from doing something you want to do in order to keep in line with your self-image. Another term for this is self-sabotage and most people don't realise they are doing it because they are unaware of their own internal affirmations and how they are affecting their lives.

For example, someone with a core belief that they don't deserve to be happy or are not good enough, will always attract or create situations that prove this belief to be true. They may have this internal self-image that they are the type of person who never gets what they really want and that nothing really works out for them.

In relationships, this person might self-sabotage by choosing partners that don't treat them well, or will stay in unhappy situations because they think they will feel even worse if their situation changes. Despite being unhappy, they will tell themselves things like, "I can't get anyone better", "I don't deserve better", "I can't meet anyone else", "This is the best I can do". Or, they will walk away from a good relationship because deep down they don't feel good enough to be with that person. They may tell themselves that they're not ready for commitment or that the timing isn't right, whilst ignoring the fact that they were happy with their partner.

In work, they may turn down a promotion they would be great at and continue to stay where they are, despite wanting to progress in their career. They will convince themselves that it was the right choice with excuses like, "It wasn't the right time", "I'm not ready", "Someone else can do a better job", "I'm happy where I am".

Another example of this is when people lose a lot of weight but end up putting it all back on a year or two later.

This is down to the fact that although they have changed their physical appearance, they have not changed their internal self-image. They look different on the outside; however, if their internal affirmation is still that they are overweight, then their self-image will continue to be a version of themselves that needs to lose weight. Despite their results, their actions and decisions will begin to change until they revert back to this internal self-image.

This is why you will see a lot of posts about "if you change your inside, your outside will change." If their belief is still, "I am overweight," they will unknowingly do things like stop working out or over-eat until their outside world reflects their internal self-image and is is why people fall off track.

Picture a thick rubber band, like the ones used for working out. Whenever you stretch them, they ping back to their original length. Now imagine that your self-image is like this rubber band; whenever you stretch it (by changing something), it eventually pings back. The only way to change things is to change the actual structure of the band, i.e., change your self-image.

Consciously, we may want a better life, want to do all the things we enjoy and have all the things we think will make us happy, but if our core beliefs contradict what we want, we will always do things that fall in line with our self-image and will rarely deviate from it.

It may seem strange that anyone would do the complete opposite of what they want to, but most people are shielded from the fact that they are holding themselves back and self-sabotaging with excuses they tell themselves to feel better about their actions. These excuses come from the ego and conceal themselves as innocent thoughts that help you to convince yourself that you made the right choices, even if those choices don't bring you what you truly want.

The Comfort Zone

WHY WE PLAY IT SAFE

Your comfort zone is a behavioural space in which your actions reflect routines and patterns that minimise the risk of you experiencing stressful situations. In your day to day life, whenever you do something that is within your comfort zone, you will make the choice or take the action that feels like the more secure or easier option. Understand that when you make a decision or do something that is within the boundaries of this space, you are always doing things that are in line with the self-image.

Anytime you decide to try something new, you are going against this image and your subconscious doesn't like this because you become more vulnerable to the risk of feeling disappointment and emotional discomfort. Your subconscious and your ego work together to keep you in your comfort zone by making sure your decisions and actions always reflect your self-image.

This is the reason why it can feel so challenging to create change and why unwanted cycles are often repeated. Actions and decisions that lie within this behavioural space are always easier, which is why at the time, they feel like a better choice. This is why people stay stuck in their old habits or routines and are afraid of change, because anytime they try to take action or do anything differently, they experience feelings of dread, fear and uncertainty. These feelings, though temporary, make the action more difficult to do and, therefore, a lot of people end up choosing the safer option of giving up and doing nothing.

Going for what you want requires you to go against your self-image, which is always going to feel like the more daunting, risky, scary choice. This is why so many people are afraid or unwilling to try new things. It's from these feelings of fear created by the subconscious mind to keep you in your 'safe place'. It doesn't care if you might end up loving what you try; it won't let you take that risk.

"If you want different, you have to do different."

Everything that you want to have right now, that you don't have, is waiting for you outside of your comfort zone. If you feel frustrated that you haven't received what you want and feel stuck in an endless cycle where nothing seems to change no matter how hard you try, it's because your actions are still based on your current self-image. Your thoughts, behaviours and actions are still aligned with your subconscious beliefs instead of your conscious wants.

So, in order to change your life and break your bad habits, you have to change internally by coming out of your comfort zone and doing the things that contradict these limiting beliefs. If you don't, you will always be stuck in the same cycle of negative repeating patterns and situations.

The diagram below represents your comfort zone; everything inside the circle is based on your current self-image. All the decisions you've made up until this point are in this circle. Outside of this circle is everything you want but seem to be struggling to get. It contains the actions and decisions you need to make in order to make changes to your life. Your 'conscious wants' are here, along with the version of you that can obtain these desires.

Every time you try to cross over your comfort zone boundary, your subconscious will try to stop you with feelings of fear.

Now imagine that you step out to do the thing you're afraid to do. Picture yourself crossing this boundary. The circle begins to expand and you reach the new things that you want. The more you challenge yourself by doing something new and going against your fears and your current self-image, you grow and evolve until you become the version of you that is sitting outside your comfort zone. When this happens, this becomes your new comfort zone and everything outside of that will become your new goals and wants.

Anytime you feel like you want to go back into your comfortable place, remember that everything you want is outside of it. If you step back in, you walk away from the life you really want and stay stuck in the place you've always known, filled with the same experiences, situations, circumstances and outcomes.

COMFORT ZONE
- Procrastination
- Emotional wounds
- Your current self image
- Things that feel easy to do
- The same cycles and patterns
- Everything you have in your life right now
- Unwillingness to try anything new
- Self-limiting beliefs
- Fear of change

ACTIONS OUTSIDE YOUR COMFORT ZONE
- Growth
- Self-awareness
- Fulfilling Career
- Positive Mindset
- New Experiences
- New Self-image
- Everything you want but don't have right now
- Positive change
- Healed Emotional Wounds
- Happy Relationships
- New Skills

The Ego

YOUR EGO IS NOT YOUR AMIGO

The ego is the conscious thought or voice in your head that justifies your decisions and actions. They're based on what your fears and subconscious beliefs are. It is always trying to get you to do things that match your self-image, regardless of what you actually want to do.

It plays a role in masking your self-sabotage.

For example, you may want to leave your job and start up a new business, but if your core belief is that you are not good enough, your ego will tell you all the reasons why it's not a good idea to leave your job right now and make you feel too afraid to take the leap.

You may find yourself thinking things like:

"I can't do it."

"It's too risky."

"It's not the right time."

"I don't have enough time."

"I should have started sooner."

"The market is too saturated right now."

"I'd be wasting all the time I've spent working for this company."

The ego will create excuses to help you justify your actions and make you feel better about your decisions, despite them going against what you might actually want. They conceal the core reason for your self-sabotaging decisions to prevent you from feeling the emotional discomfort of facing the truth of your actions. I like to call these the "Ego Excuses."

In this example, the ego stops you from realising that the real reason you are not leaving your job and starting your dream business is really caused by a fear of failure, created by a belief that you are not good enough that is buried deep in your subconscious mind and constantly on repeat.

Your subconscious beliefs will always try to protect you from doing anything that could cause you emotional distress and keep you in your comfort zone. Your ego will support your subconscious by hiding the real reason for your feelings, stopping you from having what you truly want. It's kind of like that friend who only tells you what you want to hear instead of what you need to hear for your own benefit.

So how does this affect your consistency?

Take a moment to think about the things you have given up on in the past and why.

Why did you struggle to stay consistent? What reasons did you tell yourself and were they really justified?

When you become aware of the fact that you are not your thoughts, you will be able to recognise when you are making ego excuses and allowing your current subconscious belief to limit you. It will make you take responsibility for your actions and regain control of your thoughts and your life. Thus, making it easier for you to step out of your comfort zone to create change. This is when you can begin to analyse your current habits and step outside of your usual patterns to make the real important changes in your life.

Ego Excuses

HOW THE EGO KEEPS YOU IN YOUR COMFORT ZONE

You will always want to procrastinate on anything that is difficult, boring, unpleasant, stressful or overwhelming. When the subconscious mind tries to protect you from this emotional distress, it makes you fear or dread the tasks you have to do, to the point where you don't do them at all. Worse still, most of the time, people don't realise they are allowing this self-sabotage to happen. As the subconscious creates fear, ego excuses hide this fact and stop you from taking responsibility for the fact that you are choosing not to do something that will get you closer to your goal.

In this chapter, I will share with you the common ego excuses that keep you in denial and stop you from taking responsibility for your choices. Once you learn them, you will be able to recognise when you're self-sabotaging, take the steps required to overcome these excuses and prevent them from holding you back.

Procrastination

EGO EXCUSES THAT CAUSE PROCRASTINATION

1. "I don't feel like it."

So many people wait until they 'feel like' doing something before they actually do it. They use the excuse that because they don't feel like doing the task, it must either mean that it's not the right time or they are not meant to do it. If you live your life like this, you will never do or achieve the things you really want. You won't stay consistent because you put your actions into the hands of fate by telling yourself that if you don't feel like doing a particular thing, it must be because you're not meant to do it.

Come to an understanding that you are ***never*** going to feel like it.

Whether it's working on your side hustle, going to the gym or getting the train to meet your friend, it's always going to feel a lot easier to do nothing instead. You may feel like you'd rather sit at home in your Pj's and binge-watch Netflix whilst snacking on popcorn, but as easy and enjoyable as it may feel to do nothing, this type of habit will never get you what you want or where you want.

The side hustle will never become your main moneymaker.

The healthy, fit, toned body you want won't appear after a family size packet of crisps.

The memories of great times with your friends won't exist.

And the fun of trying something new and exciting will never be experienced.

You can only have these things when you put in some effort, take risks and make yourself do things even when you don't feel like doing them. Not only that, when you do something that you initially didn't feel like doing, it's never as dreadful as you thought. You end up having a great time and feel glad you did it. So, if you don't want to end up looking back one day wishing you had kept going, stop waiting until you feel like doing something and just go do it.

2. "I'm too tired."

This is also a very common excuse I hear and it's funny because it's such an easy one to fix. If you're too tired, get more sleep! Yes, it is that simple!

We all know this, yet I'm willing to bet that most of you at some point stayed up late to watch tv, or play on your phone. And whilst I'm not saying that you shouldn't do that, if you want to feel more energised and less sleep deprived, make a conscious effort to get more sleep. Go to bed an hour earlier, start eating foods that nourish your body instead of foods that make you feel sluggish and lastly, stop saying you are too tired. Every time you say it, you are affirming this statement and making it real. The more you say it, the more you will have experiences that make you feel like you have no energy. You'll then start to believe it until it becomes another self-limiting belief.

Your brain is taking in lots of information throughout the day and it can only process so much on a conscious level, so whatever you are thinking about is what it will focus on. If you are always thinking about how tired you are, your brain will automatically filter out anything that contradicts this. All you will start to see and experience is situations that confirm that you are too tired.

Have you ever heard someone say they had 10 hours of sleep but still feel tired? Technically, the body has had enough sleep and should feel energised, so why doesn't it? Because the brain in the body is only focussed on the feeling of tiredness, so the body adapts to this thought.

Still don't believe me? Take a moment and think about the best meal you've ever had.

How did it smell?

What did it look like?

What did it taste like?

Imagine you are eating this meal right now and keep that image in your head.

If you are salivating at the thought, then you just used visualisation to trick the brain into reacting to what you think about.

Your body doesn't know that your favourite meal isn't in front of you right now, it doesn't know you can't taste, smell or eat it. But it reacts as if that meal is in front of you because you thought about it and you kept that thought in your mind long enough for your body to react.

This works the exact same way when you think and say that you are too tired all the time. Your body will react accordingly.

3. "I don't have time."

This is by far the most common excuse used when someone is trying to justify why they aren't doing something they say they want to do.

And whilst I understand that everyone's situation is different and some people may have more time than others, it doesn't mean you can't find *some* time to work towards something you want. Even if you don't spend as many hours as someone else on something, it doesn't mean that the time you spend on your goals isn't valuable.

It all comes down to how you choose to prioritise your time.

Do you have time to scroll through Instagram or TikTok?

Do you have time to watch television when you are home?

Do you have time to play video games or post on Facebook?

If you have time to do these things, then you can carve out some time during your day to work towards something you want. It doesn't matter if it's 15 minutes or 2 hours; if you can work on your goals daily, your work will add up and you will make more progress than if you never got started.

If you have just realised that you are someone who uses lack of time as an excuse, stop it now. Remember what I mentioned in the last section about constantly saying you are too tired? The same thing happens when you say you don't have time.

The more you think or repeat this "I don't have time" statement, the less time you will think you have. You will begin to self-sabotage by creating other tasks that you think you need to do first and that take up more time, but aren't a priority.

One of my coaching clients was having an issue with getting her divorce documents complete for her lawyers. She said her issue was finding the time to do them. When asked what she had done so far, her reply was, "Nothing". I asked her to list all of the tasks that she still had to do as well as the ones she had been prioritising. We were able to establish that the work she had been prioritising, i.e., cleaning the house, working on her online business, and focusing on her health, had become a form of procrastination. Whilst they were important tasks, they were not time-sensitive and did not need to be done before she could complete her paperwork for her lawyers.

By acknowledging this form of procrastination, we were able to realise that the reason for my client's lack of productivity in this area was caused more by her feelings of shame about her divorce and the overwhelm and dread of doing the work, as opposed to her not having the time to do it. We were able to organise her time and use some of it to work on her paperwork for the lawyers. Within two weeks, she had managed to complete all of the paperwork she had been struggling with for the last 2 months. Moreover, she was even able to do some work towards the other tasks that had previously been getting in the way.

As difficult as it can be to admit when you are making ego excuses, once you do, it makes them easier to address.

Now, you may be thinking that you do more than others do and that's why you don't have as much time to spend how you like. Just know that there is someone out there with more to do than you and they are managing to do it. If you are reading this and feeling guilty, please know that this is not my intention. I just want to highlight the fact that it *is* possible to do everything you want to do – it's just a matter of how you choose to spend your day.

Decide on what is important to you and then allocate time to it. If you don't, you might wake up one day feeling like you've wasted your days and wishing that you had done more.

"Doing just 1% of something is better than doing 20% of nothing"

4. "I can't do it"

As soon as you affirm that you can't do something, you take the responsibility off of yourself. Saying "I can't" suggests that you are completely powerless when it comes to what you are trying to do. You are essentially declaring that the outcome of your situation is not your fault. And if it's not your fault, you don't need to do anything about it, and giving up becomes easier to accept. You might find yourself saying things like, "I'm just not that type of person" or "I wasn't born or brought up that way, which is why I can't do it". By putting the blame onto uncontrollable circumstances, you don't have to take any responsibility for the fact that you are afraid or unwilling to find alternative solutions to your problem.

Instead of thinking of ways to overcome your setbacks, you give up and reside in the fact that it wasn't meant for you. When in actual fact, you have the ability to adapt at any time and the only thing that differentiates you from someone who "can do it", comes down to your thoughts and beliefs about yourself.

"I can't do it" is often a replacement for much less limiting beliefs that would require you to be honest with yourself in a way that might not feel great to admit, for example:

"I don't know how to do this" *(We all like to think we know everything)*

"It hasn't worked out how I expected, I may need to change something" *(Admitting to disappointment)*

"My plan is taking longer than expected" *(I'm worried that it won't work out because nothing is happening)*

When you read these statements, you'll notice that they are not final; solutions or other methods can be found if you choose to look for them.

As the subconscious is trying to protect you from admitting to these less limiting beliefs, it feels easier to blame your circumstances on factors outside of your control. This way, you can give up easily and no extra work is required from you to change your situation.

"You are what you think."

5. "It's not working"

If you can only picture things working out in a certain way and don't leave any room for an alternative outcome and things don't happen exactly how you expected, you feel more inclined to stop trying. Many people will give up at the first hurdle because things didn't turn out the way they wanted. Instead of changing their game plan, they change their goal or give up on it altogether. When something hasn't gone as you'd hope, the feelings of disappointment take over and because you feel hurt, the subconscious makes you want to retreat back into your comfort zone, to stop you from feeling even more disappointment.

So, although it is important to stay focussed on your goals, it is also important to accept when they don't go exactly to plan. That way you won't feel so shocked and upset if it happens, by accepting the unexpected outcome, you'll be able to handle any situation that arises and keep moving forward towards the things you want.

If you want to stop hiding behind this ego excuse, the best thing you can do is get comfortable with the fact that things will not always go your way; in fact, expect them not to. When you do this, you will become less rigid in how you do things. You will get into the habit of trying new methods and instead of giving up on your goal, you'll give up on the idea of things having to go precisely how you'd like. As a result, you will become less narrow-minded in how things should happen and more open to new ideas and experiences.

"If something hasn't worked out the way you planned, don't change the goal — change the method."

6. "No one else is doing it"

When you're working towards something that no one else understands or can relate to, it can feel lonely and isolating. You can be left wondering if what you are doing is even a good idea. This can make you more likely to give up on your dreams because no one likes to feel alone and disconnected from everyone around them. Lack of accountability becomes a result of this. If there is no one close to you, supporting you or encouraging you, you will feel less motivated to try, let alone keep going.

When friends or family don't understand or support your goals, it can be extremely disheartening, which then causes self-doubt. It makes you lose faith in yourself and what you are doing, especially if someone you care about is telling you that you're making the wrong choice. You end up thinking, "Nobody else is doing what I am doing, maybe I am wrong" or "I should be content with what I have because everyone else is".

Whenever your friends or family are not supporting you, expand your circle and be around people whose goals, mindset and ideas match yours. It doesn't mean you have to disown your current circle, it just means you have other people that have similar interests to you and can offer support and advice.

For example, if you have a weight loss goal, but all your friends aren't interested in eating healthy or working out, they are more likely to encourage you to break your diet or skip the gym. The problem with this is that these friends may not know how to support you because they don't have an understanding of why you want to make a change.

They may say things like, "You're fine just as you are", "Just have it, one slice won't hurt", or even "You're no fun anymore since you went on this diet". It's easy to give in to peer pressure, especially when you're in social situations that tempt you into doing things that contradict your goals. If you were to surround yourself with someone who likes to keep fit and eat healthy, they would encourage and motivate you to stay on track, which is more in line with your goals.

If you are working on a side hustle and as a result have to limit your socialising time, your friends might complain that you don't have time for them or tell you that you are lucky and that you don't need to do anything else because you are already doing well. They may not understand why you are doing what you are doing and that's because they are not you. Only you know what you really want and what type of person you want to become.

When you step out of your comfort zone and start to change your habits, actions and ways of thinking, it automatically forces the people around you to change. They now have to adapt to this new version of you and they may not like that because they are not ready to change. This can be one of the reasons why your loved ones don't support your journey; it's their resistance to their own change that is being projected onto you.

As frustrating as it can be, whenever this happens, try to have more understanding towards them. Everyone is at different stages in their lives and unlike you, they may not be ready or willing to change themselves yet, and they may never be. It doesn't mean that you have to give up on your own goals because of it. By just realising that you are both at different stages will make you less affected by their unsupportive actions or words. Know that their resistance to what you are doing doesn't actually have a lot to do with you, but more to do with their resistance to their own change.

"Don't take advice from someone who isn't living the life you want."

The Formula

THE CONSISTENCY FORMULA

I am now going to share my consistency formula with you. This simple, yet effective method has helped me to write and publish four books, gain more confidence and self-belief, lose 22 pounds and keep working towards my goals, even when people were telling me to give up because I would fail.

Each of the following steps plays an important part in building better habits, changing your self-limiting beliefs and staying consistent. When you combine them, you make reaching your goals and becoming the person you want much more attainable.

1. Goals and Habits

If you don't know who you are, how will you know what will make you happy? If you don't know what will make you happy, how will you know what to do next?

It's important to get clear about what you want and about what type of person you want to become, because if you're about to change your lifestyle, it has to be for something that's going to be worth changing for, otherwise you'll find it very difficult to stay consistent.

This is why the first step is to have a clear idea of what you want to achieve and of the type of person you want to become. When I talk about who you want to become, I mean it in terms of what kind of person that would be living the life you are striving for.

What would this type of person do every day? What lifestyle choices would they make? How would they interact with others? How would they react to situations and what would they spend their time doing? When you think about these things, you create a more realistic image of what your life is going to look like.

This is good for two reasons:

1. It lets you see what habits you will need to adopt to reach your goal, so that you can decide whether it's really what you want or not.
2. When you get started on the work, you won't feel as overwhelmed with what is actually involved. Most people will have a goal that they want to achieve but don't think about the commitment it will take or about how the change is going to impact their lives, so when they get started, they are not prepared and become overwhelmed by the work involved. This causes them to give up easily as well as become afraid of trying anything new.

"If you don't set a destination into your Sat Nav, it won't know where to take you."

Success isn't down to luck or skill alone, it comes down to the daily habits you adopt that will either get you closer to your goal or take you further away from it. So if your habits don't align, you have to change them until they do.

An unhealthy, overweight person can become fit and healthy when they consistently make healthier choices, just like someone who is fit and healthy can become overweight over time if they constantly eat junk food and don't exercise. It all comes down to what they spend the majority of their time doing.

When you get clear about what you want and who you want to become, it makes it easier to know what habits you need to adopt. This is why it is important to create new habits when you set a goal; the combination is what is going to help you to succeed.

Regardless of what you are working towards, you will always have some moments when you feel like giving up.

The key thing to remember here is that it is okay to not feel okay at times. It doesn't mean you're not doing well, it doesn't mean you won't get to where you want and it doesn't mean you should give up on your dream. This is why it is so important to set a clear goal in your mind, so that on days where you feel like this, you can think back to your goal and remember exactly what you are working towards and why you want it in the first place.

Many people are stuck in decision limbo because they don't know what they want or they are too afraid to admit it, because to do so would mean they are admitting that they are not happy with their current situation, and they need to take action to change it. This can be a hard pill to swallow, because it requires you to step out of your comfort zone, something we've already established that our subconscious minds don't like us to do. Indecisive people let the feeling of resistance to change keep them stuck in limbo. They know they are unhappy but are too afraid to take action and make decisions to do anything about it, and end up doing nothing at all. Indecision is one of the biggest happiness killers. Nothing can change until a decision is made and you start focusing on what you actually want. Only then can things in your life change.

If you're not sure about what you want and find it difficult to figure out, start trying new things you have never done before but always thought about doing. When you do this, you can begin to figure out what you like and eliminate what you don't. This process will eventually help you find something you are passionate about and you'll have many exciting new experiences along the way.

Goals and Habits

SETTING YOUR GOAL

1. Get clear and be honest about what you want and about the type of person you want to become.

If you have health goals you want to achieve, think about what a healthy person would do every day and what they would eat, and then think about how you can implement these habits into your current routine. Get a clear image of what your days will look like and how you will look and feel once you reach your goal.

If you only target yourself to lose weight and get fit, but don't determine how you will do it or how much you want to lose, you will struggle to do it because you haven't considered the changes you will need to make. The vagueness makes it more difficult for you to hold it in your mind on the days when you don't feel like working out or preparing a healthy meal.

If it's a business goal, it always helps to have milestones to work towards and to think about what a successful person in business would do, how they would act and what their daily routine would look like. Think about how it will feel, what your life will look like and the money you will be earning. The more specific you are at this stage, the easier it will be to break down the steps to get organised. Doing this will also give you a much more realistic timeline to reach those milestones.

If it's a personal goal such as becoming a more confident person, think about what's holding you back at the moment. What do you feel insecure about and what are some things you could do to change it? It could be that you make more effort to speak to your colleagues, improve your social skills and meet new people or even speak to a therapist or life coach to work on the things that make you feel less confident.

2. Create a statement for it, i.e., "I am a successful life coach earning 5k a month".

3. Write a letter to yourself from the future when you have achieved this goal; get specific about how your life is, how you feel, what you love.

Reading your letter will help you step into the emotion of already having what you want. The more you do this, the easier it is to get into that feeling. On the days when you don't feel like doing anything, being able to get into this energy will really help you to stay focused and can help motivate you.

4. Each morning, write down your statement at least three times and repeat it to yourself as often as possible, and read your letter every evening before you go to bed.

When you follow this, you begin to consciously direct your focus towards your goal. It will remind you of your 'Why' everyday and help you to stay consistent.

2. Plan, Plan, Plan!

Here's another reason why you need to set a goal, because without one, you cannot make a plan and without this, you are much more tempted to do nothing.

When you wake up in the morning and you don't have a set of tasks that get you closer to your goal, there's more chance of you procrastinating and allowing distractions to take you away from the work that needs to be done. If you plan out your day ahead, as soon as you wake up in the morning, you will know exactly what you have to do, making it easier to get straight to work.

The other benefit is that it reduces the chance of you becoming overwhelmed with the work required. Most people panic when they think about all the things that they have to do in order to get to where they want and don't take the step to break their goals down. They end up doing nothing as a result because they think, "I'll never be able to do all this work, so what's the point in starting".

Instead of focusing on the small tasks they can do everyday, they focus on the whole picture and allow their heads to get overloaded and stop believing they can achieve the things they want.

They convince themselves they can't do it and let their ego excuses sabotage their plans. Without a precise, realistic and manageable plan, it makes it easier to put off your start date. If these thoughts aren't shifted to more positive thoughts that are aligned with what you want to achieve, you will always repeat the same self-sabotaging cycle until your subconscious beliefs are changed.

"Even baby steps will take you places."

Most people think that in order to be successful, we have to be doing everything intensely and at super speed, 24/7. There are so many coaches/influencers that talk about the "hustle" and how you have to sacrifice a, b and c to get what you want. And whilst I do believe we have to work hard to a degree, the message that you must give up everything enjoyable in order to get everything you want can be a very negative message that can put you off working towards something altogether. It creates more overwhelm and dread for how much work will be required, making you less likely to enjoy the process and more inclined to give up.

When the message is that you have to sacrifice everything you enjoy in order to get what you want, it can leave very little incentive to keep going. This can also cause procrastination and failure to get started in the first place. If you try to do everything all in a day, you risk the chance of mentally and physically burning yourself out. You may be able to run at this type of speed and energy for a little while and you get a lot done in that time but you *will* burnout and may end up taking even more time to recover.

When you plan realistically and choose to take several little steps, you can still enjoy your life, whilst working towards creating a better one for yourself. The little steps will accumulate over time and the process will feel so easy that you won't have any trouble continuing until you have reached your goal.

Have you ever dreaded going to a workout class only to feel amazing afterwards? Ever saved for months to buy something you really wanted? Or stuck it out at University, despite wanting to quit several times?

When you take small but consistent steps forward, the feeling of accomplishment when you get there makes the little sacrifices worth it.

Plan, plan, plan

CREATING YOUR PLAN

1. Think about the daily habits you want to adopt that will get you closer to your goal and closer to the type of person you want to become.
2. Then take those smaller goals and break them down again, and keep doing this until you have a series of baby steps.

For example, if your goal is to set up your own salon business, the initial breakdown to your smaller goals might look like this.

Set Up Business

1. Market Research
2. Location/Shop
3. Treatments/Structure
4. Business Name
5. Shop Design
6. Legalities
7. Launch Date

Then your next smaller breakdowns could look like this:

Market Research
1. Find good locations
2. Search Local Competitors
3. Find out what treatments are popular
4. Clientele

Location/Shop
1. Determine shop requirements (size, rooms, etc.)
2. Allocate budget for shop refit and equipment
3. Search for shops to rent in choice location
4. Contact estate agents to arrange viewings
5. Confirm move-in date
6. Plan launch date

Treatments/Structure
1. Set operational hours
2. Staff requirements
3. Decide what treatments to offer
4. Equipment needed
5. Pricing

Then, taking these sub-categories, you can break them down even further into daily tasks. The key is to reduce the size of the task down to a bitesize amount that won't take long to do. You make each step so easy that you will be able to carry out the tasks on a daily basis without too much thought. It may not feel like a lot of work and it may seem like you're not doing much but soon you'll notice how quickly the work you've done adds up.

Think of your goal as if you are building a 1000 piece jigsaw puzzle. When you first get started, it may look like an endless task and you may wonder how you will get it all done. But if you spend some time separating the pieces into categories such as ends, corners, middles and then colours, it becomes a bit easier. You could view this part as the planning stage. Then as you place each piece, you build a bigger part of the puzzle. It may only be a few pieces at a time, like your manageable daily tasks, but over time, the bigger picture will start to unfold and you'll start to see the progress you are making. It's the exact same with your plan. It may not look like you're doing much at first, but if you can stay consistent and be patient, you will start to see how much you are actually achieving.

EXERCISE

Executing Your Plan Daily

1. Allocate a realistic amount of time you can use to work on your plan each day and decide what type of habit you would like to adopt or improve on.
2. Take your broken down goal and split it into smaller goals. Create daily tasks that will take no longer than your allocated time to work on your goal. For example, if you have decided you can manage 30 minutes per day, create tasks that take no longer than 30 minutes.
3. Every evening, create a To-do list for the next day.
4. Throughout the day, run through your to-do list and check off everything you have done that day. Not only will you feel super productive but the sense of achievement will help you see how capable you are and should make you feel great.

If you haven't finished everything, don't worry, just move it to the next day's goals. When you get a good routine with this, you will find your days are more fulfilled and you'll feel happier knowing you're making the most of your time.

Tip: There will always be something that's more fun or easier to do, but if it doesn't align with what you want for your future, make sure it doesn't take all of your day and set aside some time to work on what you really want.

I wrote this book whilst I was on my daily commute to work. I would spend the 45 minute journey writing and then on the way back I would watch a Netflix episode. I could have probably worked on my book on the journey home and gotten even more work done; however, I chose not to because the amount I was doing was manageable enough that it didn't feel like work. Finding this balance was what helped me to stay consistent, and finish this book, whilst still being able to enjoy some time for myself. When you find a pace and workload that works for you, it stops feeling like work. You'll find it easier to stay consistent and start to build habits that align with what you want.

3. Prove Yourself Wrong

Remember when I talked about how self-limiting beliefs play a big part in your lack of consistency? This part of the formula is how you begin to change those beliefs to ones that actually work for you.

Self-Limiting Belief *– subconscious ideas/images we have about ourselves. They come in the form of the negative thoughts or ego excuses that cause us to self-sabotage.*

Think about something you want to do, but you haven't managed to because of a self-limiting belief.

Let's say you want to get up an hour early to do a workout before work, but you find yourself thinking, "I am not a morning person, I could never get up at that time".

Whenever you say something like this, you limit yourself and are confirming that you cannot get up in the morning. However, if you can wake up early just one time, technically your "I am not a morning person" statement would be incorrect because you were in actual fact capable of waking up early, even if it was just for one day.

This is how you prove yourself wrong and start to unravel your negative thoughts to change your self-limiting beliefs so that you can stop getting in your own way.

By proving yourself wrong, you have stepped out of your comfort zone for the first time. Once you do this however, your subconscious will try to inhibit you even more with other negative thoughts. Now, instead of telling yourself you are not a morning person and can't wake up, you might find new thoughts like, "I only woke up that time because I wasn't as tired as usual" or "That was just a fluke, I could never do that again".

In other words, this will keep happening until you are so used to breaking away from your negative thoughts, that it no longer feels difficult to do. This is how you expand your comfort zone and evolve into a newer version of yourself.

These negative thoughts will keep coming and it will feel easier to believe them than to believe that you can change them, but the more you can prove yourself wrong and prove these thoughts wrong, i.e., continue to wake up at 5am and work out, these thoughts will begin to fade away and be replaced with what will be your new truth – "I am a morning person and I can wake up at 5am. I am already doing it!"

You are the one who decides if you will get up at 5am to work out, not your thoughts. You already know you can do it, it's just a matter of ***if*** you will choose to do it again.

When you become consciously aware of this, you will start to realise that you are only restricted in the mind and not the body. You will understand that you have control over what type of person you want to be and that it has nothing to do with fate, destiny or whatever has happened in the past. It has everything to do with who you believe you are and what you believe you are capable of. Start to change your beliefs and you will start to break your old habits to become the type of person that would be living the life you want.

"When you change your inner world, your outer world begins to change."

Another way of understanding this is to picture a glass with a dark liquid inside of it. Imagine that this dark liquid represents your self-limiting belief. Now imagine that every time you prove your negative belief wrong, you add a drop of water to the glass.

The first drop you add may not make a difference to the colour of the liquid; it may be very slightly diluted, but it's still dark. In other words, your self-limiting belief is still apparent. But the more drops of water you add to this dark liquid, the lighter it will get, until one day there's more water than dark liquid inside the glass. Every time you prove yourself wrong, you dilute that belief more and more, until one day, your belief in yourself is greater than your self-limiting belief. This is when positive thoughts become your more predominant thoughts.

EXERCISE

Proving Yourself Wrong

1. Become aware of a negative thought or ego excuse that has been stopping you from doing something you want to do.
2. Take a few moments to think about whether it's true. For example, if your excuse is, "I don't have time", then map out your day and see whether you can fit time in somewhere to carry out the task.
3. Once you accept that you have been allowing these beliefs to hold you back, make the decision to carry out the task one day this week or something that will get you close to it so you can begin to prove yourself wrong and break down your limiting beliefs.

For example, if you want to wake up at 5am to work out, but you currently sleep until 8am, start off by waking up one hour earlier. Once you become used to this and have made it a habit, build up the hours until you can wake up at 5am to work out.

4. Continue building on these little tasks until you have created a habit of consistently doing the work. Little by little, this will add up and one day when you look back at how far you have come, it will reaffirm how capable you

are. It will increase your confidence within yourself and motivate you to keep striving towards what you want.

4. Trust

"There's no point in working on my passions, they won't lead to anything"

"There's no point in speaking to my manager, it won't change anything"

"There's no point in going to the gym, I won't lose weight anyway"

"There's no point in going out tonight, I will never meet anyone"

What is the point in doing something that isn't going to make a difference?

When we feel this way, it leaves very little incentive to keep doing something that doesn't feel like it's working. No one is going to feel motivated enough to continuously do something if they don't believe they will get any results. So if you feel this way towards the goal you're working towards, there's a pretty good chance you'll give up before achieving it.

There may be times when what you're doing isn't working, but if you've only just started and you're feeling that way, it's more likely down to a lack of trust.

Whether it's trust in the process, trust in what you are working towards, trust in yourself or your ability, if you don't believe that you can achieve your goal or have what you want, then you're going to find it difficult to keep doing the work.

This is where proving yourself wrong comes in. The more you do it, the more you strengthen your belief by focussing on the proof and start to trust in the process.

It's also about changing your thoughts with simple mindset shifts that will help you to build your trust.

"Would you rather live in a house that took one day to build, or a house that took one year?"

EXERCISE

LEARNING TO TRUST

In the following chapters, I share with you the things you can do whenever you feel your faith wavering and need a little encouragement to keep going.

Lack of Trust in the Process

Whenever you find yourself questioning why you haven't seen any results yet, instead of thinking that it's because your idea isn't good enough and that things aren't working out, allow yourself to believe that it's just because you haven't stayed consistent for long enough yet. Recognise that when you feel this way, it's your lack of trust in the process that's causing these emotions. Instead of telling yourself that it's not working, tell yourself that everything is happening in the right way, at the right time.

Remember that changing your life takes time, and most of the time, we expect things to happen right away – which they never do.

So, if you're in the habit of asking why nothing has happened yet, hang in there and keep going. If you give up, you'll never know just how close you could have been to achieving your goal.

If you've been working at something for some time and you still aren't getting any results, it may be time to change your tactics and try another method. It doesn't mean you have to give up on your idea completely; it just means that there may be a better way for you to do things.

Practice this way of thinking and get used to the idea that your plan may not go exactly the way you hoped it would. When you are more open to changes like this, you become more open to other opportunities and ideas that might get you closer to your goal.

"If what you're doing still isn't working, change your method, not your goal!"

LOSS OF BELIEF IN YOUR IDEA

Self-doubt is another symptom of a lack of trust. When you stop believing in yourself, you stop believing in what you are doing. It can be difficult to stay motivated with this type of mindset. Whenever you find yourself doubting your ideas and doubting whether you can achieve this goal, this thought always comforts me.

Don't let the fact that you haven't seen results yet make you stop what you are doing. In order for something to work, you need to believe it will, so when you start to question yourself, strengthen your belief by remembering that you started on this journey for a reason.

Remember that there is already a part of you that knows you are able to achieve this goal. It was the part of you that got you started in the first place. Your belief was strong enough to turn a thought into an idea and then into an action. Therefore, it will be enough to push you through the days where your trust starts to falter.

"If you have already started working towards your goal, know that a part of you at that moment believed in your idea, believed you could do it and that it would work."

NEGATIVE THOUGHTS

Whenever negative thoughts invade your head and try to get you to stop what you are doing (remember, your subconscious is always trying to keep you in your comfort zone), I find that talking back to them helps.

Question any negative thought you have and ask if it's true. Think of the things you are already doing which disprove your negative thoughts. When you start to do this, you will see how untrue these thoughts are and begin to separate yourself from them. You start to understand that you are not your thoughts, that you can take control of what you think about. You don't have to listen to them; you can change them and start choosing more positive thoughts.

Give it a try the next time you find negative thoughts trying to take control and stop you from doing something you want.

"Whether you think you can or can't, you are right."

One Week Plan

GETTING STARTED

Now that you have the formula for consistency, it's time to get to work…but sometimes, that can be the hardest part.

If you haven't started yet, it can be difficult because it requires you to take action and do something you have never done before and the first step can be the scariest. Also, once you start, you'll have made a commitment towards your goals and if you give up now, it will feel more disappointing than if you never got started in the first place.

You can research and plan all you want, but until you take physical action and get going, ***nothing*** is going to change. This is why the next part of this book is going to give you a pre-made plan to get you moving forward.

You already have the steps to set your goal and create your plan, so now I'm going to help you get started with this one-week goal prep to get you out of your procrastination funk and excited about your new venture.

You'll notice that I haven't used specific days of the week, this is because most people are in the habit of waiting until Monday to start something new, but the reality is that you can get started at any time. "Waiting until Monday" is another form of procrastination that can be changed if you start to prove the belief wrong.

Day 1 - Clean up your space

Day 2 - Get organised

Day 3 - Decide on your goal

Day 4 - Break down your plan

Day 5 - Create a schedule

Day 6 - Create your affirmation and a vision board (optional)

Day 7 - Next day to-do list and get to bed early

"Nothing will change unless you change"

DAY 1: CLEANING UP YOUR SPACE

If your surroundings are cluttered and messy, your headspace will also feel cluttered and messy, making it more difficult to organise your tasks and get anything done. Having a clean and tidy work space can make all the difference.

This is why I recommend you doing a clear out of anything you no longer have use for and organising the space around you. Everything including ourselves is made up of energy, so if you have a lot of things you no longer use cluttering up your home, it can leave a stagnant energy in the air.

It can make starting a new project feel less exciting, which will leave you feeling less motivated. It's also a great excuse to procrastinate ("I have too much to do around the house and have no time to work on my goals this week"). So when you tidy up your space, you won't be able to make any excuses about having too many other things to do that prevent you from getting started.

You will have clean, fresh surroundings, meaning your headspace will also be nice and clear for you to get started on your goal.

DAY 2: GET EVERYTHING YOU NEED

Use this day to pick up all the tools, equipment, stationary, etc. that you will need in order to execute your plan. I always pick up a fresh notebook to write down all my ideas and another one for my daily to-do list. This will also stop you from procrastinating by telling yourself, "I can't do anything this week, because I don't have all the things I need".

Buying some new materials will get you excited and feeling good about starting something new. Remember, your subconscious will always try to stop you because it wants you to stay comfortable, so doing things that get you feeling happy and excited about making a change will keep your motivational momentum going.

DAY 3: YOUR GOAL

Today, you are going to get very clear about what it is you truly want. Take some time to think about it and be honest with yourself. Don't go for the goal that you think is achievable because it won't be what you really want. It will be something you feel afraid to admit you'd love or are afraid to work towards because that will be your true desire.

The goal is going to look different for everyone. For some, it may be something like starting their own business, for others it may be to get promoted at work, buy a house, or even just drop a dress size. Whatever it is, it's a goal that will be specific to your needs.

For me, it was to complete my first book and get it published.

At the time, this was my main goal, I didn't have any thoughts about starting a podcast or writing a second, third or fourth book – that all came afterwards. If you have lots of things you want to achieve, but have struggled in the past to get any of it done, pick one goal to focus on and start with that. Only move onto something else once you have completed it.

If you had told me at the time of writing my first book that I would also be writing three others, along with starting my own podcast show, I would have freaked out at the thought of having so much to do. I probably wouldn't have done any of it.

This is why it is important to get clear about what you want, so you can direct all your focus on achieving it. This will help you to stay consistent because you won't get sidetracked with all the other things you also want to do.

Have you ever tried cooking a meal whilst preparing all the ingredients at the same time?

There is so much to do; you have to wash the vegetables, peel and cut them, prepare the meat, get the oven on, create a sauce, set the table, prep and make the rice and you have to do it all so that everything is ready at the same time. Then once you're done, your kitchen looks as though it's been ransacked by racoons.

Then there's the other way you can cook. You can prepare everything first and clean the dishes as you go along, so that when it comes to cooking, everything is ready for you. This method is so much more organised; it makes the process easier and there's less mess and stress involved.

Approach your goals in the same way. The cooked meal is that vision you have of your life with all your goals achieved; each part of the process is a goal that will take you closer to your dream life. If you try to reach every goal at the same time, it can get overwhelming, messy and the end result might not be so great. But if you focus on one goal at a time, each task gets your undivided attention. Always think quality over quantity.

DAY 4: YOUR PLAN

Today is the day you are going to break your goal down into a plan that will fit in with your current lifestyle.

1. Decide how much time each day you can spend working on your goals.
2. Break your goal down into smaller goals and tasks that you can do on a daily basis (More details in the chapter on planning).
3. Don't try to overdo it in the beginning; make your daily tasks manageable.
4. After a month, you can review your progress and add more tasks if you feel like you want to.
5. Track your progress and celebrate the mini milestones.

DAY 5: YOUR SCHEDULE

Being organised is going to help you to stay consistent, which is why the next step is to plan out your week.

Take time to map out what days and times you are working, so that you can set aside a realistic amount of time to work on your goals. Getting organised is going to stop you from procrastinating and using the excuse that you're too busy to do some goal work because you will already have set aside the time to do it.

Setting the intention is a mental commitment to do something. This, along with your structured plan will help you stay on track and not allow distractions to get in your way.

DAY 6: AFFIRMATION

Today you will spend some time creating the perfect affirmation that aligns with what you want. Be specific and make sure you word it in a way that flows easily because this affirmation is going to be with you until you reach your goal.

Examples:

Health

"I am so happy and grateful now that I have reached my goal weight by making healthy choices everyday and exercising regularly. I look and feel amazing."

Business

"I am so happy and grateful now that I have started my own business and it is running successfully. I get to wake up every day and do what I love."

Self-Worth

"I am so happy and grateful now that I recognise my worth. I am filled with confidence and love the person I am."

Home

"I am so happy and grateful now that I am a homeowner. Once I made the decision to buy my own house, I found a way to do it."

Once you have your perfect affirmation, write it out on paper, change your phone wallpaper to it and memorise it.

Every day, set aside some time for you to write out your affirmation at least 3 times. As you are writing it, allow the thoughts of your goal to be the main focus, and then imagine how it will feel once you achieve it. Allow these feelings to take over and get lost in the image, let yourself feel excited about your goal and excited about working towards it.

I recommend doing this in the morning to start on a high note. Anytime you feel doubt or negativity creeping in, go back to your affirmation and read it (out loud if possible) until you start to feel excited, happy, good feelings again. When we feel negative because our day isn't going well, it can be difficult not to focus on what's gone wrong, but the more you do this, the worse your day will get. By turning your focus back onto what you want, you shift your thoughts and energy away from negative situations.

Whenever your day isn't going well, bring your focus back to your goal – the thing you ***do*** want. If you have a job that is unfulfilling but pays the bills while you build your own business, as frustrating as it can be, remind yourself of your main goal and know that your current job is helping you to live as you work towards what you really want. Start to feel grateful that you have a job that affords you the time to work on your dream business. This will make your days go by easier, knowing that it's all going towards a bigger picture.

DAY 7: NEXT DAY TO-DO LIST AND GETTING TO BED EARLY

This week of prep has been building you up to this moment – tomorrow is the day you start working towards achieving your goals.

Today's task is to create your to-do list for the next day.

Write down everything you have to do tomorrow in the order you have to do it in and set times next to each task. Be sure to include things such as your commute, working, lunch, etc. This is going to help you throughout the day when you don't feel like doing anything. Knowing that you have a task on your list will make you more likely to focus on getting it done. Throughout the day, be sure to score off the tasks you have completed.

This exercise will help you see how productive you are; it will make you feel good and more likely to want to keep going.

This list is the best way to build a new habit and get more work done, so make sure you don't skip it. This is something you will do every evening before bed. I always do this in the evening because it means that as soon as I wake up, I know exactly what I'm doing. It saves time and reduces the risk of you telling yourself you'll get started tomorrow because you don't feel like it. By allocating specific times to your tasks, you train your brain to realise that you do have enough time to do the things you want and when you see that they won't actually take too long to complete. This will make you feel more inclined to carry out the task so that you can score it off your list.

For example, you might have a pile of clean washing that you've been meaning to put away, but haven't gotten around to yet. You might think it will take forever, that you have more important things to be doing and that you just can't be bothered. Having it on your list and seeing that it will only take about 10 minutes to complete will make you think, "What's 10 minutes?" Once you have completed the task, you'll not only feel good about it, but you'll start to change how you utilise your time. You'll see that you actually have more time than you think you do and that your tasks don't take as long as you think. You'll find that you can get a lot more done.

It may seem like a lot to begin with, but over time this process will become second nature and then it'll get to the point where you just do everything without having to plan it. You will have created a new habit and a new way of living.

Lastly, make sure you get to bed early, so that you are well-rested in the morning and ready to really get started on changing your life!

Staying Motivated

USEFUL TIPS TO KEEP YOU GOING

Visualisations

Whenever you feel like you can't be bothered to do something or your negative thoughts try to prevent you from being productive, try to visualise the task before you do it.

When you imagine yourself doing it, think of it as an easy, smooth process and then think about how good it will feel to get it done. Let the feelings of satisfaction take over and stay in this feeling for a while.

This should help motivate you to get started – and that's all you need!

It's just a little push to get the momentum going. Once you start, it becomes a lot easier to keep moving.

Most of the time, we don't do something because we think it will be difficult and that we won't enjoy it, but like most things, they never end up being as bad as we think, and we end up enjoying the benefits even more.

By focusing on the positive feeling of completing your task, instead of how awful it will be doing it, you create more of an incentive to get to work.

If you haven't consciously done visualisation before, start with something small.

A great example of this is when it comes to changing your bed sheets. It's just one of those necessary tasks that is extremely boring. I don't think anyone actually enjoys doing it, but we all know how good it feels to get into bed with fresh new sheets and how amazing we sleep. The smell of the fabric softener, the feel of crisp, clean bedding, the cosiness of getting into your bed and sinking into your pillow – it makes changing your sheets regularly so worth it!

Does that thought make you feel like changing your sheets tonight?

If so, you have just used visualisation to help motivate you.

You can use this method for anything you have to do. The more you do it, the easier it gets and the easier your tasks become.

Remember the formula… The first time you get started, you will have proved your fears and negative thoughts wrong. Then each time you have to move again, you will have a memory to refer back to. You will be able to recall how good it felt to complete your task/work. Not only do you stay consistent, expand your comfort zone and create a new habit, you build trust in your own capabilities.

'Me Time'

When you are working towards something, it can be easy to put everything and everyone else on hold until you have reached your goal. You think that you can no longer do the things you enjoy because you think you need to put all of your energy into your work. And while it's true that you need to focus on the things you want, you also need to be kind to yourself and have fun once in a while.

When I was writing my books, I had a terrible habit of shutting everyone and everything out. I believed I had to focus all my attention on my books, so much so that I let everything else slide. This went on for months until I burned out and could not bring myself to keep working. I ended up taking a break that lasted longer than it needed to and much longer than I wanted it to. I lost the momentum and motivation to work on my book and dreaded starting back up again.

This was because I created the belief that working on my book equated to not having any fun. I cut out any enjoyment whilst I was writing, because I felt like I could only have one or the other. This made it very difficult to "enjoy the process", which made it much easier for me to want to give up. The trick to staying consistent and getting back to work after taking a break, is to make the process fun, or at least not so strict that you dread going back to it, because that's when most people give up for good.

This is why "Me Time" is so important. Make sure you carve some time out to do something you enjoy and that makes you happy. You need to make the process of working enjoyable enough that you'll want to keep going, but also that it'll feel worth the small compromises you have to make to your time.

I always think there is too much pressure and too many messages on the internet, telling people that they "have" to give all of their time and energy to their goal and sacrifice everything else. Even though you do need to keep focus, you don't need to sell your soul to get what you want. You are allowed to enjoy life, whilst still working on something that will make it even better.

It's all about moderation.

You can still meet up with friends and have a drink, whilst working towards a health goal. You can have days where you want to binge a Netflix series and still work on a side hustle. You can still take a city break and have fun whilst you're working towards your goal; you don't have to wait until you are successful. It doesn't have to be all or nothing. You just have to decide that it won't be and then set aside some time just for you to do what you enjoy.

Not only will it make the process more enjoyable and realistically achievable, it will remind you of why you are working towards your goal in the first place.

Earn Your Chill Time

This is a really great way to motivate you and it makes your "Me Time" even more satisfying. Get into the habit of relaxing once you have completed your tasks for the day. This might seem daunting to begin with, but once you experience the feeling of "Me Time" after a productive day, you will realise how much more satisfying that time becomes. Knowing that you have worked towards something bigger will make you feel like you've really earned your chill time.

Get into the habit of having a treat after you have completed your tasks, when you do, you will be able to relax even more. This will feel so different to when you procrastinate and do something fun to avoid a task that needs doing because there will be nothing in the back of your mind reminding you that you still have things to do. You will have achieved everything for the day and when you sit down to do something you love, you'll find that enjoyment so much sweeter.

Mantras

I love using mantras to give a little boost of motivation.

Whenever you go to do something and a little negative "I can't do it", "I don't have enough time" or "I can't be bothered" thought comes into your head, you can instantly combat it with a more positive mantra like, "I can do it because I believe I can", "I make time for the things I want to do" or "I get to choose what I spend my energy on". When you have chosen your mantra, repeat it over and over again until it replaces your negative thought.

For me, "Keep going, you can do anything" always gets me moving. Anytime I feel like giving up or skipping a task, I repeat this until my body starts to take action and I get to work.

I used to do this a lot in the mornings when I would try to get up early to do my workout. My alarm would go off and I would think, "I'm too tired" or "I'll do it tomorrow". Then I would catch my self-sabotaging talk and refer to my mantra, "just do it Suz, it's only 30 minutes, you'll feel great afterwards". I would repeat this in my head and after a few times I'd feel motivated enough to get out of bed and start my workout. It always felt great afterwards and over time, it became easier to do. I followed the formula – Set goals, plan, prove yourself wrong and trust. Each time I proved myself wrong, my trust would strengthen until it became second nature to just get up and work out.

When you replace your negative thoughts with positive words and affirm them to yourself until you feel good, you shift your energy and become those words. This then translates into physical action, making it easier for you to actually do the task.

This will really help in the beginning of your journey and whenever you try something new. Initially, you may feel resistant to a change in your routine and it will feel easier to revert back to your old ways of doing things, but the more you can do things that are out of your routine, the more progress you will make and the more you will change your self-limiting beliefs.

To start using these mantras, you first have to become aware of your negative thoughts.

Take a notebook and jot down any negative thought you have that day, and then find a mantra that feels better than your negative thought. Then, whenever the thought comes into your head, refer to your chosen mantra and repeat it until your mood shifts.

Practice this by actively focusing on what you think about throughout the day. Anytime you catch yourself thinking a negative thought, replace that thought with an outcome you would like and repeat it until your focus shifts away from your negative thought. This will help to reprogram your brain to focus on the positive things around you.

Go For the Long Reward (Delayed Gratification)

One of the reasons why we give up on the things we want is because we don't get the results we want right away.

As a result, we do things that give us instant gratification, which doesn't last very long, and we end up giving up on things that would make us truly happy. We end up sacrificing long-term fulfilment for short-term happiness because the process is easier and quicker.

Examples include:

O Binge eating junk food because it makes you feel good at the time, but messes up your long-term goal of becoming healthier and losing weight.

O Using all your money to buy clothes, bags, shoes, cars, etc., which give the appearance of success and wealth instead of creating actual wealth. Buying these things and having them will feel good momentarily, but it's usually not long until you're looking for the next upgrade and chasing that 'feel good feeling' of buying something new. You end up sacrificing your long-term goal of having financial freedom to do what you want by settling for a lesser reward.

- Settling for an unhappy relationship to avoid feeling lonely, instead of doing the inner work to become more self-assured and comfortable being on your own, until you meet someone who is right for you. You end up sacrificing the opportunity to become more emotionally mature and independent as well as risk the chance of being with someone who is not right for you and can meet your needs.

- Staying in a job you don't like because it's good money and you've done it for years instead of following your dreams and doing something you will love. You sacrifice job fulfilment for comfort and security. Now, I'm not saying everyone should quit their jobs right away, but remember we spend over half our lives in work. So, if you find yourself miserable every day and you dread going in, it might be time to ask yourself why you do it and if it's worth half of your life.

These options might not seem so bad right now and you may feel okay with where you are, but they may make you feel uneasy in the future when you find yourself looking back on today and wishing you had done things differently.

Imagine where you would like to be 5 years from now. Is what you're currently doing going to get you there?

If not, what could you do differently to ensure you don't look back with regret?

The satisfaction of eating junk food passes very quickly. The clothes, cars, shoes and watches go out of fashion. The relationships will fall apart or become so unfulfilling and unbearable that temporary loneliness won't seem like such a bad thing. And the job you stayed in that you hated could no longer exist.

I can't tell you whether your situation is like these examples; only you will know that. My point is that if you only focus on the instant rewards and the short-term satisfaction, your happiness will also only be short-lived.

So take some time to access all areas in your life. Think about what you're happy with and what you would change. Do you have any deal breakers? Are there any areas where you are settling for less than you deserve?

If so, it might be time to do something about it.

Hold out and work towards your truly fulfilling long-term goal. It might take longer to achieve, but your happiness will last a lot longer.

Work On Your Own Time Frame

Comparison is the quickest way to create self-doubt. If you are always focussed on what others are doing and how far ahead they are compared to you, you will never feel good enough. Stop comparing yourself to others and remember that we are all unique.

Everyone has different rates of growth and are at different stages in life. We are all on our own timeframe. Start to accept this and you will realise that it doesn't matter how much more someone has done or whether they are more successful than you are right now. You will get there too – as long as you stay focussed on your own path.

Know that how someone else is doing is not only none of your business, but it has nothing to do with how well you are doing. The only comparison should be with who you were yesterday, last week, last month or last year. Whenever you find yourself comparing yourself to others and feeling the sting of envy, look at how far you have come on your own journey.

Bring the focus back to you.

"If you are always looking over someone else's path, you will lose focus on your own"

Summary

Now that you have the formula for consistency, the steps to help you get started and the tools and methods to help you keep going, you can apply them to any area of your life that you are dissatisfied with and want to improve on.

When you start to do this, you start making changes that will have an ever-lasting effect on your life.

This simple formula is the key to unlocking your potential and putting a stop to your self-sabotaging ways.

All you have to do is make a start and keep going.

This book wasn't written to make you work non-stop like a robot. It was created to make the journey to your goals easier, give you tools to make the process more manageable and to make you less likely to give up altogether. Remember that you can achieve anything you put your mind to – there is no time or age limit. As long as you keep going, keep focused on your goal and don't let self-doubt get in the way, you will achieve anything you want.

Lastly, remember to be kind to yourself. Although I've made it easier for you to stay consistent, know that sometimes you are not going to feel like doing anything and there will be times where you give in to that feeling – and that's okay! The main thing is that once you're feeling better, you get back to work.

Good luck, you've got this!

"It doesn't matter how little you've done; if it's the best you can do for today, then it's enough!"

Printed in Great Britain
by Amazon